IN AN IDEAL WO
I'D NOT BE MU

IN AN IDEAL WORLD
I'D NOT BE MURDERED

Chaucer Cameron

Published 2021 by Against the Grain Poetry Press
againstthegrainpoetrypress.wordpress.com

ISBN 978-1-9163447-4-7

Printed by 4edge Limited
4edge.co.uk

Contents

To my dearest Helen
&
[   ]

128 Farleigh Road

I find him at the bottom of the stairs, the strange thing is
his eyes are blue with flecks of grey. I could have sworn
they were brown, a dull sort of brown, but then again
the mask, which often hid his eyes and *always* hid his face.
Apart from one-time years ago when I caught him naked
and alone. Now in death that face looks so serene,
clean almost. I'd often worried that the rubber marks
on his jawline, forehead and just beneath his eyes,
would pit his skin so deep he'd be scarred for life.
But here we are, just he and I gazing at each other
the way dead people do when caught together intimately.
One thing troubles me. I say this in a whisper so not to disturb
the dust that's gathered. *How did this come to be?*
This flat, these walls, they're crawling with dead girls.

I know the rules: no names, no dates, just numbers.

I'll Teach You How to Switchblades

You know I carry switchblades
like the way YOU wear stilettos.

When Crystal told stories
I learned to keep quite still.
I knew she wouldn't mean to
but she'd lash me with her tongue
if I so much as hinted, she was wrong.

You know I carry switchblades, she said,
then paused to judge effect.

You know I've never liked you.
You think you're something special
but you're nothing really, are you?
You're just like the rest of us.
I've heard you with the punters –
you're no escort, you're a whore.

The Green

The bus stopped
at the edge of The Green.

It was a dark winter evening
Ellen still had a twenty-minute walk home.

Bears ... wild boars maybe.
That rustling crack closing in
must be animal.

It took three days to discover the body,
reporters said it was hard to identify –

devoured mostly.

Body Marks

Wrist

Fat slag, he'd called me.
She held up both her wrists
to display cuts and blisters.
Ceci n'est pas une pipe –
it's my time bomb.

(Caprice)

Elbows and Knees

Scrapes and grazes,
then like a cow in heat,
munched my way through
balls and dick –
sucked the life right out of it.

(Eve)

Outside Forearm

Cut it on a bottle/
hidden/ in the grass.
That's what I told her/ anyway.

Mum was always kind
ready with a bandage/
stitched me up/

put her hand/ between my legs.
Stitched me up/ stitched me up/
stitched me up/

(Grace)

Inside Forearm

I am a palimpsest, she said,
beneath this rose tattoo – a barcode –

(Morgan)

Love

Ash held off a stab wound
through her laugh.
It developed overnight
into a grating hound-noise.

Words weren't easy after that.
But sometimes *love* was useful,
alerting those around her,
a forewarning of attack.

(Ash)

King's Cross Café (I)

Crystal would always talk about her body
A body bought and sold ages so much faster
as if it wasn't real – wounds – scars –
than the general population.
She'd often throw in random facts like that.

Cartoons

It's funny what you think of when you've had a near miss/ I
don't think my nose is broken/ could've been much worse/
no time to check it out/ it doesn't hurt/ anyway.

It's funny what you think of/ when you're gagging/ for your life
when you hear the car doors/ click/
when the music is turned up/ and you put on your disguise.

Tonight/ it was the Flintstones/ I watched them as a kid/ you
can watch it on YouTube/ it's a sort of animation/
they used to call them cartoons/ but I can't tell the difference.

The Flintstones were a family/ there was Fred and Barney/
Wilma/ and a Betty/ I had a crush on Betty/
what a beauty/ lovely legs/ she was a real animation.

Fred and Wilma had a kid/ every family had a kid/ named their
daughter Pebbles/ oh/ there was a Bamm-Bamm/ I'm forgetting/
Bamm-Bamm/ they found him on the doorstep/ then took him in.

I loved that show/ I loved the way they loved their kids/
it's funny what you think of/ when you've got a dodgy punter/
bloody Flintstones/ bloody Pebbles/ hell/ a broken nose.

(Peyton)

14

Be Nice

I was blamed for shagging.
I'm not sure what's wrong with it.
Tricia's done it twice, she said.
She's sixteen, I'm nearly eight.

#Cam Girl 23

was found in an armadillo pose
hunched over the keyboard, hooked to a screen:
her index finger worn down to the bone,
tap, tap, tapping – put years on her.

(Cam)

Administration

Amy worked in admin,
met clients in the office.
Evenings it was shorthand.

Ladders always featured,
as did stockings and a stockroom.
Balanced on a middle rung.

Oh hello, Mr Carter.
Yes, I've nearly finished.
It's so nice of you to come, and so quickly.

(Amy)

Hooked

I remember standing on a street corner,
eating BLT on rye,
thinking about my fluid intake.

But despite my thirst, despite Taboo,
I aimed for the Three Crowns,
ordered fruit juice (nearly).

It was an ordinary evening, drear, overcast.
Outside, the traffic was building;
diesel fumes circled the inside of my nostrils.

Air, I needed it.
Exited (or tried to).

It was raining, so I called a cab,
considered my options,
bent at the edges.

The traffic was static – the traffic eased –
the traffic was at a standstill –
the traffic flowed nicely.

The taxi turned right – past
Clissold Park, to …

It had been a long time since I'd
been in that part of the city.
I remember how quickly evenings turned dark,

how my cigarettes slid between seats,
how my fingers, not as slim,
not as deft as they once were,

reached deep into the crease
deep down.

King's Cross Café (II)

If they knew I was a whore..., she used to say.
She had issues, kept secrets, mostly from her family.
I often think of Crystal and wonder
what we would have done if we'd had a different life.
We spent a lot of time together when she wasn't high.

Erotic

Back in '82
there were
no poles to
slither down.
Olympic
moves
would have
filled my
pint glass
twenty times
or more.

But now
my
movements
jar to a
jiggle,
twitch
and split
as I
elevate my
torso
while thinking
of that
night
I'd hailed
a cab to Hoxton.

I was late,
it was raining,
I'd argued
over money.

I'd had
too much
to drink.
That meant 'yes'.
Did it?

Sodomized
they called it
but I don't
remember details.
The papers said
no underwear,
reported every
action
as erotic.

Now
back on stage
I lift
my buttocks
high,
bend knees,
open thighs,
shuffle sideways,
head turned
this way,
that way.

Someone jeers,
someone touches

while my eyes
reflect their cash
and ten-pound
plastic cards.

It's an act,
the art
of stripping;
it's an art
the act
of stripping –
I can never
quite decide.

But here,
tonight,
a pint glass
does the rounds,
half-full:
loose change
that clanks
against the sides
is a sign
I've lost.
Skin no longer
tight against my frame

fixes me
at half price.
Doesn't it?

My dressing
room
has dwindled
to toilet size.
No door locks,
grime-smeared
floor tiles
cracked.
I cower
in a corner
until the owner
comes to check.

This time
he shows
pity,
dresses me
in finery,
takes me
to his table;

he likes
the meat,
the tuck, tuck,
twist of me.

He likes
to see
the light
in my
acid eyes
go out
just before
they
close.

Coup de Maître

I lay you on your back, twist off your claw-legs,
crack them with a heavy implement.
I will not allow you to shatter into small pieces, yet.

I will extract the bones of you,
place them with care into a metal bowl.
I will insert thumbs on the base of your body
push upwards to release you from your carapace.

I will pull away and discard your lungs –
they are only *dead man's fingers;*
you know them intimately, don't you?

I will press your mouth with such force that it snaps
from its shell. I will raid your stomach-sac,
cut you in half, scoop out the meat of you,
fork out the white from your carcass.

You will be left hollow, your cavities
will shimmer thinly, rocking back and forth,
open, empty, ready to be stuffed, dressed, put on show.

Then we will dine. You will be picked, hand-held,
lifted high on a fork, ready to be savoured
by tongue, swallowed down into the gut,
where you'll rest for a moment, before clawing
your way back through every orifice imaginable.

Taking the Piss

I'm a work of art, I'm a sex magnet,
just look at these, she said,

as she pulled down her begonias
from the shelf –

see how they flourish when you piss on 'em;
makes a girl feel good, don't it?

Dad used to say taking the piss
was a way to shut out the mess
in my head.

(Trixie)

Trixie is A Whore

I think I adore her – well you would,
wouldn't you? She's so hot, so damned cute.

The piss – she takes mine, I let it go right on cue.
No dribbles, no tang, not that I can detect.

She says she's sixteen, but I don't believe her.
She's tiny, still tight; I reckon she's younger,

which suits me just fine – I can get her to piss
with the tip of my finger.

Rate her – 8/10

Hina Needs Swabbing

Hina's cheap tonight; she's been damaged.
There are tears in her silicone – cracks around her genitals.

She's done well; she's lasted six months
but her left breast has a puncture,
her hips are overstretched – anus slightly ruptured.

She was favoured by a trainee gynaecologist
who used her every Monday; now he wants a change.

She was specially designed for him – marked with his initials.
She has no teeth or tongue, but flick her
on both nipples – she'll orgasm when you come.

Hina says nothing – she hangs naked from her hook.

Introductions

Night. A dimly lit street. An almost empty café. Dull, bland interior –
brown wooden chairs, a brown leather sofa, a dark brown tub chair
in the corner. A male waiter with scraggy, scrapped-back hair stands
behind the counter. Crystal is sitting by the window of the café, while
another woman sits on the floor at her feet. A young woman lies
asleep, slumped on a broken, battered bean bag at the back of the
room. She has covered up her legs with an ochre cardigan.

'That is Jaen,' says Crystal, pointing towards the sleeping woman.
'J A E N, not Jayne with a Y, or even plain Jane, but, J A E N, for
god's sake, talk about making life hard.'

Crystal lights a cigarette.

'Jaen Foster, she calls herself; look, she's even got it tattooed on
her knuckles.

I had a daughter once – she was fostered; well, she was for a
while. I was only allowed to see her on Saturdays. Then I found
out – some, oh so nice, adoptive family got her. She's not
fostered, she's adopted, and her name is, anyone's guess.
Anonymous. A-NON-Y-MOUS.

It won't be the name I gave her though, will it? They won't tell
me what it is – her name, I mean. I'll never know what they
chose until she's old enough to find me, if she even bothers –
will I? And then I'll have to wait and even then – she'll still be
A-non-y-mous, Bare-ly There. Anyway, there she is, that's Jaen
Foster, J A E N.'

Crystal gets up, stretches and orders a coffee, just for herself.

'You weren't here when she turned up last week, were you? She
was in a right state – told us some story that she'd sort of had a
baby! A miscarriage, abortion, I can't remember which.
Whatever, the foetus ended up in the dustbin. Is that a criminal
offence? I mean, if it's flushed down the toilet, no one would be
any the wiser, would they? Just a cramp or two, a bleed, a full
stop.

It's not that hard to flush a foetus down the loo, unless you listen to
that claptrap from that pro-life lot, the ones that make you
feel like shit. They stand there with their banners, with their
slimy little posters, and the way they call them *babies*, *little
people*, *small humans*, *beating hearts*. And yeah, I guess,
how could you really flush a little beating heart down the toilet
and not commit suicide when you can't live with the flashbacks?'

King's Cross Café (III)

The next time I saw Crystal
she hadn't had a fix.
I want to be a journalist, she said,
I'm fucking getting out of this.
She was always asking questions,
always wanting the story.

In an Ideal World I'd Not Be Murdered

In an ideal world I'd buy a bigger place, a place where us girls could work together. There's safety in numbers. Not afraid of getting busted or being murdered.

I refuse to compromise my safety, said Crystal, inviting strangers back to her room. But nights were always hard for Crystal, *there's a safety in jeopardy, ain't there?*

Crystal loved art. Her bedsit covered in posters from the sixties. Blondes, semi nudes, mostly murdered women. Her favourite chair, just a knock-off imitation, she called her Keeler chair.

Crystal could've been a hoarder, but in fact she was a hooker. She was lucky, never murdered, she understood erasure, turned it into artforms, pinned it to the walls.

Crystal knew what she wanted and that was somewhere quiet, *but not so quiet I get murdered.* Then she'd giggle, try to disarm you with laughter, but not really.

I Will Leave You for a Moment While I Trade

Outside the road is eerie;
street corners are calling.
You're hunched inside a doorway
behind you lights still strobe.

Black and white, white and black,
your skin reflected in car headlights.
Two black bombers go down nicely
but it's extra cold tonight so a microdot
will do the trick –

I will leave you for a moment,
in the doorway, doubled over
as you insert two finger widths
of tampon into your vagina,
so no slow bleeding shows;
the cramps will ease with Valium.

I'll leave you on your knees while
I go to check the river –

it's busy on the Thames;
Canary Wharf, I hear it sing.

Acknowledgements

Firstly, I'd like to thank the editors at Against the Grain, Jessica Mookherjee, Karen Dennison and Abegail Morley, for having such faith and trust in my writing and who were willing to take me on.

I'd also like to thank the groups I've been involved with over the years. *Covent Garden Stanza*, for their help and support in, 'saying the difficult thing', *Worcester Stanza*, *The Hours Group* and *Poetry Swindon* for their encouragement and commitment, and *Strange Cargo*, for their friendship.

Thank you to Sissy Doutsiou, director of Athens Poetry Festival for inviting me to read this work there. And to Silver Street, for giving me my first UK opportunity to perform part of this work.

I'm especially grateful to Jacqueline Saphra, for her kindness, patience and unwavering faith in my work. And to Sarah Leavesley for her insightful comments.

Special thanks to Sabrina Mahfouz whose work I deeply cherish and will carry with me always – *your work was the spark that lit a fire under this book.*

There have been so many people that have literally been a lifeline while I've been writing this material. In particular David Clarke, Joelle Taylor, and further afield Zoë Brigley and Patricia Smith, whose work has given me permission to write the 'harder parts'.

None of this would have happened without the help and support of all the organisations that I've engaged with over the years. A huge thank you to the incredibly brave people involved, some who are still with us ... and some In Memoriam: Ellen G, T Cassidy, Malcolm, Joan/John, Pat – so many more.

Last but not least to my adoptive mum and dad Nancy and William (I miss you) & to my birth mum and dad Doreen and Bob.

Finally, I *need* to acknowledge the now deceased, hospital therapist, Roger/David Tio Liyong. Roger was one of the reasons why I entered prostitution. RIP. I've survived.